Portulans

JASON SOMMER

Portulans

THE UNIVERSITY OF CHICAGO PRESS

Chicago and London

The University of Chicago Press, Chicago 60637
The University of Chicago Press, Ltd., London
© 2021 by The University of Chicago
Published 2021
Printed in the United States of America

30 29 28 27 26 25 24 23 22 21   1 2 3 4 5

ISBN-13: 978-0-226-73739-3 (paper)
ISBN-13: 978-0-226-73742-3 (e-book)
DOI: https://doi.org/10.7208/chicago/9780226737423.001.0001

Library of Congress Cataloging-in-Publication Data

Names: Sommer, Jason, author.
Title: Portulans / Jason Sommer.
Description: Chicago : The University of Chicago Press, 2021. | Series: Phoenix poets
Identifiers: LCCN 2020013381 | ISBN 9780226737393 (paperback) | ISBN 9780226737423 (ebook)
Subjects: LCGFT: Poetry.
Classification: LCC PS3569.O6532 P67 2021 | DDC 811/.54—dc23
LC record available at https://lccn.loc.gov/2020013381

♾ This paper meets the requirements of ANSI/NISO Z39.48-1992 (Permanence of Paper).

for Allison

. . . traditionally are described as itineraries rather than as maps: diagrams organized around the still subject-centered or existential journey of the traveler, along which various significant key features are marked—oases, mountain ranges, rivers, monuments, and the like. The most highly developed form of such diagrams is the nautical itinerary, the sea chart, or *portulans*, where coastal features are noted for the use of Mediterranean navigators.
—Fredric Jameson, *Postmodernism, or, The Cultural Logic of Late Capitalism*

CONTENTS

ACKNOWLEDGMENTS

Grateful acknowledgment is due to the editors of the following journals in which these poems, sometimes in different form, first appeared:

> *Cincinnati Review*: "Children Wearing My Shoes"
> *The Forward*: "What Men Want"
> *Delmar*: "The Most I Took Back from a Dream"
> *Ploughshares*: "Grudge"
> *River Styx*: "Multiverse"
> *Sou'wester*: "Changing the Script" and "Incident at the
> Mother's"

My thanks also to *Poetry Daily* for their posting of "Children Wearing My Shoes" and "Incident at the Mother's."

My deepest appreciation goes to Alan Shapiro, Chuck Sweetman, Jerry Harp, Jane Wayne, Rich Moran, and Kevin Stevens for years of careful reading and encouragement.

Portulans

SOUL

Some notions he has slumping half asleep
in a reading chair, this time drowsing over
Le Morte D'Arthur. As he's felt newly old
of late—so badly needing one or two
ultimate answers, wanting, for example,
to know he might not die so absolutely,
which would be the soul's department if
he has one, and if he does, surely there's
a way to sense it—ping the satellite
and test reception. The metaphor is all
wrong, of course. It's inner space he's after,
though news of an immortal part would greatly
unify the field: the spark of life,
in persons as in stars. A record also
isn't it, more than our animating fire,
a manifest of spiritual condition?:
Knights lost in error Gawain dreams as black
bulls, milling starved. Tethered in pasture, a pure
white pair graze near to one with a single spot
of black, the trio fit to quest the Grail.

A perfect time for metaphysics now—
the night against the window, and he turns
the last light out, not to make the glass
into a mirror. Darkness settles grainy,
loose-woven, faint wash of moon and streetlamp—

around his chair, small sounds of various sizes—
aggregate, pebble and stone—that constitute
the silence hereabouts and at this hour.
He draws himself upright for meditation—
a staticky first rush of thoughts, too much
the noise of mental strife, now trying hard,
the bearing down, if he's to find there's something
other than the clutter—down, down through,
down past the themes made out of memory—
he as abandoned; he as abandoner—
past all the incidents of memory—
through personality and temperament.
A path might start near conscience, or maybe
the neighborhood of dreaming, but leading where?
A stratum of essence—fundamental, ghostly
also, with earthly personhood subtracted?
Never a blank, though, where the sin-tally
is kept (imbalance sheet of deficits,
yet he will seldom think of a head accountant).
The only part so pure it can be sullied
is stand-in for the body in receipt
of its hereafter, so a residue
of self remains, or who exactly will
get suitable comeuppance or reward?
One version of believing anyway,
while in another that undying portion
becomes the last word in spare parts, a spare
entirety—and everything he is and has
gone through will be gone, shed, burnt away
eventually, presumably, to clear
for a come-back to the world as someone else.

Cleared then, but utterly. Couldn't one
be partly cleared beforehand, please, and know
about it, even for a passing moment?
The old desire for pardon—and it burns
always a little to recall the reasons,
black marks of his, and he no good at all
at self-forgiveness. The two of them together
trapped in that house, and his side of the cruelties,
most of the cruelties on his side, he would
have to admit and wished he never thought of.
And that's commission, there was plenty else. . . .

A wave comes in to end the reverie:
beta, alpha, quick tide turn of the brain,
an erasure in the now and here that washes
away the line of thought. What had it been?
Where was he? The mind's buoyant gravities—
what goes down must come up again. He's rising
already with nothing but an image for
himself, a gas bubble drifting upward
out of a sulfurous vent in the ocean floor.

THE EXPEDITION

Beyond the failure to return at all,
or having managed bare survival,
addled past reliable report,

always the chance you would have come up empty,
back to the surface and from afar
with nothingness to show, never

in your lifetime to know
that what you'd done had been of use
to you or anyone, nothing

transformed but moments that made hours,
years, your record for persistence
evidence to doubt your skill.

And yet that final route you took
would seem the selfsame one once traveled by
the greatest of the journeyers

whose names at least remain to us,
signed in their own hands—manifest
and log—claims made on their behalf,

the truth of certain ancient maps, borne out.

Your sketches over photographs
sought to recover only outlines

but make inspired sense to those
who read phrenology on ocean floors,
who see in shadowed dents and mounds

within the clean geometry
of precincts—tomb and temple and palace—
a perimeter of habitation, houses

vanished, even their middens carried off
on the tiny motions of the sand.

The trove-sites emptied long before

the land's descent and sea's rise,
other raiders leaving precious laden,
not having to ration time by air

or flee that temblor that brought you up
so quickly when whatever might
have been went down toward center Earth.

The one shapely stone in your clutch
the whole way back, so like a figurine,
with suspect crosshatch scratching also,

was never artifactual enough.
Too long turned in the lathe of the sea to trust.
Still, your account alone inclined

so many to belief that you must be
allowed as having had a sighting,
albeit, as it must be, unconfirmed.

THE MOST I TOOK BACK FROM A DREAM

The ghost sensations in the limb that's gone
are by report the ordinary ones.
Though free variations come when we shed
entire bodies in the sleeping bed,
we seldom feel as we have never done.

So when I tumbled from a nightmare roof,
I woke before arriving at a truth
not known, though losing what seemed consciousness
before I struck the ground felt more or less
familiar as the sudden downward route,

which ended in an interregnum
awake in bed, before I fell again
into a sleep. By morning I had flown,
swooping over a landscape of pocked stone
in County Clare. First kited by the wind

sweeping me helpless from the Burren to Moher
and out to sea, I soon began to go where
I inclined: downward after downcast eyes,
but also looking upward I would rise.
How could I disbelieve it? I was there,

aloft, approving Moher's precipice
and Burren rock for visionary practice.
As if this were the place I would awaken,
armed only with that skill which must be taken
from dreams, the spirit steered me bodiless.

IN THE BASEMENT IS THE PREVIOUS CULTURE

And the ones previous to it, *ad finitum*,
     in no order, heaped, leaned, and shelved
          as for a sorting likely destined
never to occur, portions of collections once
considered entire and items no longer
      answering the question "how?" But what
        might they be?
              A Zenith radio at nadir
for certain, from the era of the ear.

The man descending to the superseded
     objects to see what else
         might have returned to value
              has come halfway now to the landing
by hand tools hung in an outline
of themselves. There are no words
     beneath the shape of things:
         hammer that is still the dream dreamt
            for the fist, the digits of the pliers,
equal and opposing and in steel.
With the stairs' turn, what he goes down to
     rises up before him.
         Against the western wall, for instance,
           the tiers of lumber up on bricks, where are visible—

strips of fichu along with scraps of tulle
among the rags that nest a weather vane
rooster, propped against a bucket brimful
of pulleys in a fruit crate with a biplane
pictured one end. A concertina's bellows
drape the other. On the isinglass pane
of an unhinged stove door, piled in a willow
basket, are printed circuits and a thin chain

linked to a stem on an adjacent gas lamp's
branch, above brass fig leaves. Just below,
a tipped box fans out an avalanche
of bills, billets-doux, some cellophane
packets: one showing Burkina Faso's stamps
that had been Volta, one Vichy's that was France.

As he enters the crooked aisle
between the zinc sink and a Fender
            bass amp, an upright mangle and steamer trunk,
                the iron helmet of the furnace starts up
                        in one of its fierce intermittencies,
shows fire through the slats
of its visor, lights up a drawing
            by an early person penciled low
                on the parged fieldstone wall,
                        a child's glyph of stick figures
joining hands, male
and female, possibly, probably bipedal,
            hardly noted anymore.

After the surveyor's tripod,
                    the architrave and stair-spindles in
a staved umbrella stand,
the treadle sewing machine
          table—ship's-wheel barometer in
                    miniature, astrolabe in replica
                              on it beside the great globe itself
in rounded cardboard—
the channel narrows.

     He sidles by
                    a toboggan on sawhorses, turntable on toboggan.
                              The mountainous still life of slave
and master cylinders, motherboard, magneto,
churn handle, has a bookend at the summit,
          its planes braced by the figure of a lounging coolie,
                    and all of it contained in an orphan drawer
                              on a suitcase on valise on portmanteau
on *National Geographic* magazines, pillared
in stacks.
          He arrives at the metal bank of shelves.

               There is a mood in which the man will stand
                         there, moved to be eye level with the
                              crockery
of the old woman who owned the place before him,
met once in her near translucency, bent
               and bright-eyed as the goddess
                         in crone's disguise. It is a pair of
                              her earthenware planters

toward which he feels a moment as tenderly
as for the Bakelite set of brush and barrettes
      that touched the head of his own grandmother
         and are kept a little higher up.

            Particulate lies general on everything
unshielded; he shuffles across it, fallen
when there were none
      to see it fall. It would keep to the forms
         at first, like light, like shadow, like light
            snow drifted thickest near the wall,
            collecting
in declivity: powder of gypsum, powdered lime,
dust of the mortar and the stone,
      of brick of block of flesh, sifting down
         from the floor above,
            invisibly moting in the dark.
He moves to go, the dust already
on him as underfoot,
      the palatal scrape of his steps a consonant
         of the language in which his grandfather
            cleared his throat in the middle of the night,
said his prayers in the day, in Voleyn
the Jerusalem recalled
      that had gone down in fire
         to the Jerusalems beneath.
            Here is another elsewhere, and underground
nothing of Jerusalem.
Trilobite dust from the vanished
      midcontinental sea leavens the concrete
         over quake-twisted strata
            that hold the scattering

of worked flint and chert,
and out of the mill of waters,
      implements of shell or perhaps
         only the shells themselves.

SATORI

The concrete lintel over the cellar door
(had I strode jauntily up on the balls of my feet
because I'd always come through clear before?)—

the bench I thought I was out from underneath
after I plugged in the plug—the fumbled box,
down from the shelf it took full stretch to reach—

these days I have been banging my head a lot.
They might be accidents, but you know what
he says of accidents, *il papa vero.*

While the sign for realization is the slap,
palm or fingers, over the brow's furrows,
it's lightly done, really just a tap,

as if to get the thinking engine to go
again, as if a gear had gotten stuck,
betokening admission of the lapse.

These blows have been a good deal harder struck,
however, than symbolic gesture, too much
for *how could I forget, I should have known,*

of course, aha, now that's where I went wrong.
So, more than sign but less than signified,
but still within the realm of metaphor,

I am clocked, conked, brained, had my bell rung,
and mean to find another figure for
what happens: maybe Janus should preside

over this going out and coming in.
The two-faced threshold god above the door,
facing this way and that, he divides

time past from future time along some thin
border that ought to lie behind the twinned
diametric faces, equidistant

precisely, I imagine it, from each.
This logic of the disembodied head
is mine, who thinks to freeze the living instant,

frantic in its passage, stopped dead
by nothing, not concussion, not the speech
of a minor god. I'd have him whisper as

freely to and fro we pass beneath
him how there needn't be for every instance
of departure a return, of how we're led

all to our own conclusions certainly
by doubtful signs—"this way to the egress"—
and prophecies: *so it may be at last*

as it's been lately in the clumsy midst.
Enough blunt force is like a sudden blast
I'd vanish in, but just a little less

will leave me in the verge's crumbly blazes
between the several forms of consciousness
I am aware of, believing vaguely there'd be

that light behind things when the world's abraded.

CHANGING THE SCRIPT

Almost at random and suddenly while walking along,
some passing flatcar in the train
of thought, I tell myself to look, to see, to be in the moment, and just
like that I am, I do.

The tired geranium in the pot by a front stoop, however limp,
blazes entirely, fills my eyes
with seeing—another state,
as in consciousness, as in grace,
not Missouri, particularly.

I have been sure I was someone for whom the great change
doesn't come—and this is not that
of course, a passage to be marked with the taking of a new name.
And who expects vision
even of a minor sort without labor—
much before—more after?

And yet and yet and yet there are those times—
and will there be others
also that I might summon
myself to, simply by the reminder
to have it be so,
a minim of spell—
the sheering over
the pitcher's lip, water falling silvery into a red bowl once—
that strike without warning?

WAKENED TO A CERTAIN KNOWLEDGE
OF A LIMITED KIND

By the long squeak of a creature or a passing vehicle braking just
beyond the three-masted stand of the yard's trees,
one possibly elm, visible through the dusty window glass
that in the slant of early light looks like the sand and fire it is.
Shadowed below the sill, a socket, and from a plug

wire dips and rises up in one direction to the nightstand's
boxy radio, way station for invisible rays, and in the other, walled up
wire to wire to more, junctioning out to wire again and again,
up and over, under, down, through until the dynamo somewhere
turning and turning out electrons, made to, by various burning means.

You, too, coming around, bed-pale, improbably ringleted, cameo
appearance, profile shifting left side, right side, left side, as you
sweep your face against the pillow, shaking your head
awake in demurral. You push up onto elbows, the wiry nimbus trembling.
By follicle shape, by uneven distribution of keratin,

by unequally opposing tension, by the decree
on other twists of protein—helices—by some first cause—presto
anyway—curls, which toss more as you lie over on your side,
still dozy, fresh from the last of morning's sleepshow. Telling the dream
has your husky first words, at least aloud, and the first thoughts

of the day that might be called such. A woman in it who looks like
your father but a woman, you insist, as if anyone were
going to doubt you, moves across a forest clearing toward you
bare-shouldered and . . . and . . . something else happened. A long pause

follows. Is there more to the story that you remember and hesitate
to say? Your eyes, though, scanning upward in their sockets,
do seem to search memory, but for what may be gone already,
gone to where it goes—wherever it came from—gone as can be imagined,
down into things, in past flesh and bark, marrow and pith, and down,
down into molecule, atom, particle, vanishing into theory.

MULTIVERSE

One of her walked right up to the door but turned
and stayed home, which of course engendered the other
one's going out. A version of the stay-
at-home for no particular reason held
her breath, causing another identical other
to come into being who kept to regular auto-
nomic functions. The latter, seated now
on a couch that is a reproduction in
the first place, listens to the radio,
which made for many listeners tuning to
an array of stations in all instances
of universes that had had Marconi

or the like. Among songs without number played
repeatedly, a single by the Beadles—
yes, with a medial *d*—the fab five—
an iridium-seller Pete Best's drumming drives,
entitled "In the Church of Bauzelaire."
And in some cosmic arrondissement, in some
dimension neighboring, and neighboring that
again and again, at diversified removes,
my very first beloved and I are still
together in so many of our forms.

That no potential future is allowed
to die except in the most local way
(that one small life that one is living) is
an article of faith among a portion
of the smart set, smartest on this Earth as well
as a hundred billion others branching onward.
A starry brilliancy of cosmologists,
astrophysicists, and provisionally godless
metaphysicians can believe with Stephen
Hawking in space-time continua
where he requires no wheelchair, breathes on his own,
speaks and sings, along with those—as must be
conceded—where things are worse for him than here.
And though it may not matter quantumly,
although it may, he has been willing to
consider in all probability a life
of being just a hair less excellent
at math and playing a passable game of tennis.

Individually and in aggregate, in wave
and particle, it may be the case
reality indulges in an endless
and continuous reproduction of souls—loosely
termed—or persons, in profusions equal
to the number of alternative outcomes
to every action in the cosmos, all
of us creators then of more of us
by stutter or by step. Even down
among the cells impossible to tell
who the original is, and when: worlds bred
and breed at every juncture—replicates
and duplicates, you in your venues, me
in mine. We sense ourselves to be like no
one else has ever been, but the ramified
are others of us who feel exactly as
we do in their existence if they exist,
not a bit less solitary, nor is the sorrow
any greater for being multiplied
out to infinity, all of which remains
unverifiable as the multiverse
itself, though déjà vu may hint at something,
muffled voices coming through the wall.

INCIDENT AT THE MOTHER'S

It would have been the last thing his mother said
to them, to him and Em, that miserable
visit, early in their marriage,
the final cutting thing
on their way out to the car,
standing before it—

after a weekend of
the usual swipes, some subtle
belittlement or other to share
between them, though more
at Em than him, he thinks,
but truly he forgets
what it was that had him

lunging at his mother—too quick for him
to be amazed at himself even—
but he did, his arms around her
back and back of the head,
the way you'd catch someone
who was falling over.

Except he was felling her,
swinging her into a waltzer's dip
and an abrupt halt, a hovering tableau
over the front of the car.

He thought he meant to say,
Just shut the hell up. Enough.
Shut up, but as he finished—

his grip, easing, became
a cradling—what came out of him
as he laid her gently down on the hood
was something from the beginning of
him, of her and him—
Shah, shah, shah,   hush—
shah, shah, shah,   hush

FOUR PHOTOS AND BRIEF CASE REPORT
FROM THE JOURNAL *SURGERY*

The man with the mark on his face begins the course
of his inaction modestly, as shown
in figure one, the first of three self-portraits
from an automated booth. Patient person,
the documented one, his face at forty-
seven takes up the most of it—moon
in a telescope lens—astronomer of astral
distance near at hand. Located left-
center equatorial, the merest
dot, a possibility, suggestion
of, the writer-doctors say, at the apex
of the nasolabial fold. Unsmiling, yet
his expression, twenty-seven years before
admission, which seems a little wry here—early
days, gets very much so later—clearly
the shadow of amusement in his eyes.

Clear and clearer what has been the star
of these, photos that aren't so much the yearly
face in black-and-white, likely on birthdays,
as what the face makes way for, the small disruption
in the fabric like a tiny wick of light
igniting an annunciating presence,
except that this is slow, slower than smolder,
already fifteen years by figure two,
twelve before admission. He's sixty-two.

What had arrived for him continues to.
The guest unbidden and made welcome is
in present guise a dimly nacreous pearl
drop pendant, in which he recognizes something,
although he may not yet be able to
identify quite what that is, beyond
that it is his—what comes for him is his,
has chosen him, and which he chooses in
return: this steadiest of burgeoning,
a life in parallel, echoing
deliberately the progress—the unfolding,
the quiet movement onward of his own.

By figure three, he tilts subtly toward
the camera his better side for picturing,
left hemiface with pebbled flesh, doubled
in size in seven years. A little hillock,
subject to erosion, low in his field
of vision now, five years before admission,
its blur will disappear into the boundary
darkness of his left eye purblind soon.
Already he can't be inside himself
just as he was, looking out on all
things there with perfect ease, the aperture
so wide it never seemed a window then.
So many days of ordinariness,
at ordinary risk, he'd moved around
the city: speeding cars he'd had to step
back from, the long drop past the guardrail—how
that spoke to him, but faintly, low in his stomach,
the way it might to anyone—as did

the urgent rhythms of the subway train
slowing to the platform where he stood.

Later followed several of the years
for which the pictures haven't been collected,
when he must either venture out or stride,
expectant of the stagey shock his presence
administers. Nothing like the cleanly
absences of amputees. So easy
to imagine them emended whole, the blank
space filled on one side by doubling what was on
the other. From him most had to look away—
his gaping lesion with its complicated
detail, beyond the reach of symmetries
and quick, complicitous imagining.

The final figure is in extreme close-up
and color, taken by someone else upon
admission to Emergency: a gory
radiance of damage where what's buried
is brought forth. Openly cartilage, sinus,
nerve, and muscle surround the nostril slot,
the pulp of the interior from upper
lip to lower eyelid on the left
as after explosion, the look of inside out.

He brings his pictures to the hospital,
a swollen wallet full. Whatever else
he'd come for, he receives a naming in
the doctors' language, something for the pain,
and has the rarity confirmed—a giant

basal cell carcinoma of the face
that's hardly ever seen, seldom left
in cultivation for as long as this one.
They would have gently said what's necessary
only but testify in their account
that it is found among the devastated
poor, the unmodern, or the insane as well
as him, whom they are law-bound to release,
who does appear sufficient to himself,
who hears no voices in his head outside
his own, judged sane enough to be allowed
refusal of all offered treatment, to leave
behind some photographs, to take his life
into the afternoon and go where none
can ever recover him, disappearing
into the deepest places of his wound.

IN THE MOMENT BEFORE THE CALL DROPS

Seems right the line between us, not properly
a line—a beam, a ray, the signal—wavers.
Sea sounds drown a sentence, abrading words
to consonants, to vowels stopped glottally
over and over in the throat of the ether,
my end at least. I can't know what you heard.

IN THEIR NATURE: A TRIO OF NEIGHBORS
IN A SIDEWALK CHAT

About the plague of them, a plague on them:
despoilers of the fruit of tree and vine—
he's biblical, her husbandman, tender
of gardens. For me, it is the builded place,
fighting the entropies throughout the body
of the house, the flow staunched here drips there and now
attic invasions, the gnawing away with those
ever-growing teeth of wood and shingle
and patience, their cries a hinge-creak trailing into
wheeze. Just their nature and the price
of living by the park, so many oaks.

And nothing, really, to raccoons, she tells us.
Where she was raised, a small farm in Missouri's
bootheel, they grew a good ten pounds and better,
could unlatch most any gate, and not just strew
the trash but carry the can a-ways, all leavings
theirs, along with what's only left unguarded.
The deft hands were never idle, nightly
at the dig and delve, the tear into
and rip open, so bold they hardly needed
cunning and masked well by country darkness.
The view into the trees around the house—
glinting back in the sweep of flashlight: paired
amber studs, eyes eyeing. No fencing
them out, no chasing them off, no killing them all.

Every now and then the boys took vengeance
of a minor sort, would set on the porch as lure
two large bowls, several feet apart—one heaped
with saltine crackers, the other brimming water.
Raccoons would come, one or two at a time,
take a cracker, bring it to the water—
the way they must if there is water, to do
a kind of washing, having that *behavior*
she read it's called—and as each does, the cracker,
dipped and rubbed, dissolves to nothing, and
the animal looks down, perplexed, at paws
a moment, the soppy fragments falling from them,
and gets right back to shuttling between the bowls.
Every attempt renews hilarity
for those who watch behind the window glass
the back-and-forth again and again until
nothing remains there to make nothing of.

I see it all, and with the little jolt
of catching sight—as of my current face
in mirrors, looking furred around in smoke:
the tonsure's shag—gray, gray swathe of beard—
knowing had I been there in the bootheel
I would have been among them, not the pranksters
but the pranked upon, under inner orders,
moving to and fro, over and over,
from one place to another, the hopeful scurry
always, only to watch at each arrival
my looked-for sustenance gone zero.

CHILDREN WEARING MY SHOES

My children have put on my shoes, the pair
of them—male and female we made them—

and boots with laces trailing; the shoes, mates—
the boy and girl not, often

contenders, all together now in this.
First, the single pair divided between them

without dispute, one shoe off, one shoe on,
feet lost in them, leg in up to the shin.

At the limp-and-drag pass in front of my chair,
I put my book down, but they turn away

before I can speak, kicking the footwear
into the corner and gone

back to the closet and back again in motley,
mad-shod, a singleton on each foot—

the separated twins of his sneaker and slipper,
her mismatch of sandals.

They crisscross the room, quickening the shuffle
to slam the heels on the floorboards,

not looking at me, not answering
to their names, intent on

the performance only, looking past
even each other, a flash of the whites of eyes

rolling, mouths open, the spooked horse look,
and a few cries of half-stifled laughter,

but the fourth wall kept intact
as they discard onto the little mound

in the corner and race out to return
with two pairs undivided on each,

old loafers on her, but he's gone formal:
processional glide of the long sedans

of gleaming black brogues, brougham
hearses. I am here, I want to tell them, still here.

HE THINKS

Not much loved, therefore he loves
less, so he thinks, but if it were
not just the way he thought it was,

and he'd surpassed the modicum,
would that have even registered
with him? Out of his fears that's one

he would admit, though it's a cover
for his full catalog, and some
more frightening by far: the terror

that what he has allowed as cause
instead was likelier effect.
He's little loved simply because

his deficits do not attract—
(provision of the natural law
pertaining to the non-elect).

And in addition there is this:
tending as he's always done
to think things over, he will over-

think things grimly also—that is—
think things are over unbegun—
think of the rest of them, the blur

of persons known, and in among
them her—certainly unsure,
but in what ways—maybe like his?—

exhausted with consideration,
held back or holding? God, then where
did that leave them, us, anyone?

TO MYSELF IN THE COMING TIME

You'll make few changes from now on,
though changes will be made, if none
you'd want. Some speak of growth, and maybe
there are those who put on wisdom
even in their final hours,
but that is on the West Coast mainly,
beneath a steady dose of sun.

For you the forecast must be plainly
cloudy. Expect declining powers,
the dictates of your genome,
although you might not notice much—
best-case scenario—the waning
being gradual enough.
(As with your dad, but not your mom.)
And your abilities were such
that access always kept you straining
and accomplishments at minimum.
So, early in a latter phase,
it may not seem unusual
if little comes of all the work.

What's to be done in any case?
Go put a sudden end to days.
Or seek out the delusional
in self-regard, that it is worth

anything for you to be doing
what you do when the alternative
no longer plausibly is screwing.
(Desire will be continual.)

It helps to have some help to live
like this, of course, others who will
reliably admire the labor
whether delighting in its fruits
or not. Your modest group of friends
will rather often urge you savor
the world, travel as substitute
for losses of concupiscence,
to grand souk and village bazaar—
the aromatics of elsewhere—
the wooden carts with spices arrayed—
bright-patterned cloth in Côte d'Ivoire—
if you can come up with the fare
before the colors in you fade.

But sense of smell will lead the way
down, and taste will go along
with scent, while on the tip of the tongue
another blankness, the word for it
escapes you, standing before some shelves
seeking something, you could swear
that objects must have moved themselves.
And you have prayed, you will admit,
desperately to remain aware.
Soon you may pray the other prayer
that is the opposite of prayer.

BILLY'S FACTS OF LIFE

Before I had the pleasure, I had the notion
pleasure had its term. So Billy taught me
at ten and he fourteen, an expert Bronx-style
merely by virtue of New York address
and near enough to tallest, biggest, most—
if good, the best; if bad, the worst, toughest. . . .

A few miles north of Yankee Stadium,
house that Ruth built, home to the champs of champs,
we loitered our route down Burnside, in and out
of stores: Yellin's to browse the comic books
or get an egg cream if we had the money
and down the aisles of Daitch Shopwell's rows
of repeating cans, boxes with cellophane
windows, and past a wood-staved pickle barrel
close by the registers, dill-scented, the green
of ghost forms in the marsh water murk.

His looks had maybe prompted his befriending
a younger boy and of another tribe
who wouldn't tease about his top front teeth,
so bucked he couldn't close his lips around them.
About which, so innocent I was, I asked
directly what had happened. He responded
with the most preposterous lie—an accident
while eating watermelon with a fork

that slipped and pried his teeth up suddenly.
This I believed as I believed the rest:

the way that babies came from women's asses
and his approximate sexology,
how something came from penises that wasn't
pee—come, he said, you called it coming,
which you could only do so many times
your whole life long, something like a thousand.

That part made sense to me, as one of those
among the group of local kids who scorned
the infinite ammo cowboy shows, where shooting
banged on and on with no reloading. I
kept count and wanted what was real for our own
gunplay (and rules for how and when the shot down
could rise again to shout *new man, new man*).

For years I offered Billy and me for the laugh,
the idea of that ration and other facts
of life. Though now, an elegy season for friends—
and one especially with whom I'd trade
Bronx stories—something seems true enough
in what Billy says of limit. I feel it in
myself, that I have passed some point or other
I couldn't track exactly, wouldn't want to,
beyond which everything is pure gift.

AT THE FRIENDS OF THE LIBRARY
LOCAL AUTHORS EVENT

Turns out that in the next seat over,
the vigorous old man and fellow author,
his accent and manner war-film German,

is Jewish, a native Austrian,
who's lately written a Holocaust memoir
about the time he spent as a partisan

in the Italian Alps. The back cover
copy of the books we have exchanged
serves as mutual introduction.

On mine he seems surprised to see
that I'm a Holocaust survivor's son.
He asks me where my father comes from.

I tell him that despite the German surname,
he's Czech, interned at first in Hungary.
And something changes in his idiom

a moment, with a shift in rhythm
that almost by itself I'd understand
as coming from the eastern European

Pale, picked up in the American
translation of his life, but he makes sure
with shibboleth: *paskudnyaks, mamzers—*

Yiddish for *sons of bitches, bastards*—
as we get talking about the war,
the Germans, and the blame, Goldhagen's

thesis, which he's all for, that brands
das volk entire accessories to murder.
I say, maybe that's not wrong,

still, what about camp guards, *Einsatzgruppen*,
the various SS, those bloodiest hands
who got away, almost all of them.

Bu-ut, just the faintest hint of singsong
Talmudic, *not those captured by our band.*
Easy to tell SS. Their blood type tattooed

underside of the left arm saved
us all a lot of useless chitchat.
These prisoners, too, were made to dig their graves.

And every one just before we'd shoot
gave a Heil Hitler and the Nazi salute,
an arm up as they fell into the ground—

what are you gonna do with people like that?
he says, shrugging like some *shtetl zeyde*,
Jewish and un-Jewish as he'd ever sound.

LOT'S DAUGHTERS

*"Let us make him drink wine tonight also, and you go and lie with him, that
we may maintain life through our father."*
—Genesis 19:34

They are going to mount their father plied with drink in quantity—
Lot, the adjunct patriarch, patriarchal in his vigor,
even under the influence, entirely under as

in blackout drunk, still able to perform, inseminate,
and disremember the performance two nights running.
The fire-working angels of their acquaintance had only begun

the fireworks when the look-back mother turned
salt stele of herself. She is pillared now on the low point
of earth for disobedience, by the shores of its saltiest sea: the dead

sea, by the dead cities from which the smoke coils as from a sacrifice
over fields salted by heaven never again to yield.

*

*"Flee for your life! Do not look behind you, nor stop anywhere in the Plain;
flee to the hills lest you be swept away."*
—Genesis 19:17

The smoldering is visible without penalty from the heights of Hebron

to the three who had been four before: *Lotsdottir* elder, *Lotsdottir*
younger, nameless otherwise, climbing behind their father
in the rocky hills. He leads, they follow for the moment.

There will be more turnings up ahead to match
what's been already. For example, the men Lot would have rescued
by turning his daughters over to the rampant gang of Sodom

turn out to be a pair of angels, who quell the rioters
at the seraphic reveal with a flash and bang
of blindness and rescue the familial lot of them instead,

and from the incineration of the city also.

*

> *He annihilated those cities and the entire Plain, and the inhabitants of*
> *the cities and the vegetation of the ground.*
> —Genesis 19:25

The girls can almost hear in the wind the lisp of the burning
as off a distant altar. Faint hiss, the faintest stench like singed hair

perhaps, as they descend into a cave in the hill country,
where they will have the further atmospherics to convince
    themselves
they are the only people in the world after a new deluge

of fire. The old ark story haunts theirs, except for the rainbow
of assurances, of course, about never again. Noah aside,
what of Uncle Abraham, how can he be disappeared—far and away
    God's

favorite man? In fact, those angels were freshly arrived from him,
first stop for every blessing, passed on sometimes to blood relations.
The errand prior was to inform him he's laughably

about to get a child at ninety-nine by wizened beauty Sarah—
wife and half-sister, by the by—his altered, covenantal loins the
    tip-off
point of descent for folk as numerous as the grains

of sand on the shore or of salt in the salt sea.

*

> *"Your name shall be Abraham, for I will make you the father of a multi-*
> *tude of nations. I will make you exceedingly fertile, and make nations of*
> *you; and kings shall come forth from you."*
> —Genesis 17:5–6

And if the angels mentioned none of this essential tribal news,
doesn't the withholding give sufficient cause for everyone believing

things were unfolding as they must in the darkness
underground? If out of delusion by deceit is the engendering
of this part of the grand design, it has them spared,

their lives if not spared everything—nor are they sparing either—
for the grandest reason misapprehension can supply—
so that the whole world may continue

in their minds where each is lone survivor
truly. Breathe a word of Abraham, and everything is his
again, and they not of the root but of the branch.

*

God remembered Abraham, and sent Lot out of the midst of the
overthrow.
  —Genesis 19:29

If Abraham were gone, it might be they were saved
for virtues of their own, just deserts for deeds or deeds
intended. The annals of hospitality, the early pages,

ought to be inscribed with the account of three
who sought to shield the angel visitors,
each according to ability—to each, then, what is deserved—

the one who would have sent them out, two virgin daughters
to the rapists in the street, the two who would have gone
in all obedience like Isaac yet to come, who will lay down

for binding on the altar and whose arrival these very angels
had annunciated as firstborn of the multitude that Abraham would
    become.
The sisters want their multiplying too and will not

lie down with their lamenting only. Plucked from Sodom's
extinction less than a week, now are they poised to show how
they might have been at home there—in the extremes

of their imaginings at least, not fleshly per se,
their minds not tuned for pleasures but obsessed with generation,
and on those stated grounds take license worthy of a Sodomite.

*

Coolly in the cave, the elder sister does the math
aloud. Everyone else subtracted, that leaves one
old father and no other male in the world, but the word

she uses—*eretz*—means either *world* or *land*, a world certainly
in the difference, a doubt right on the slippery tongue
for persons who are listening and can hear

themselves. If there is no man to quicken them in the familiar
manner, so says the elder, none like or like unto their father,
then it must be the man who is not like but is

their father, Lot. So much of logic issues out
of faulty premises here: from a cave in the first place
on the high ground, from presumptive sole survivorhood

to syllogize themselves into the company of the elect.
The righteous shall be spared; they are spared; therefore
that is what they are, who will do rightly by inclination

if they do simply what is given them to do.

*

But what they do has to have been done in a kind of fog.
And whatever way they feel they feel that way beyond reason

48

in the shock and aftershock of sudden losses: the mother;
their married sisters; so many lovely citizen children still
previous to the evil they would do;

the father who had been as he was before he granted
as substitute and ransom the use of his maiden daughters to a mob;
and also among the slavering pack no doubt a charming

devil or two they'd had an innocent eye for,
bad-boy sweetness annihilated at the sight,
the twisted faces, gape-mouthed in the general howling.

*

> *"See, I have two daughters who have not known a man. Let me bring them
> out to you, and you may do with them as you please; but do not do any-
> thing to these men, since they have come under the shelter of my roof."*
> —Genesis 19:8

Drifting to the daughters in the lingering concussion
of the miraculous barrage are the truths about the bodies:
how they may be offered up, altered, altared, rendered

salt and smoke and ash, rendered unto—in exchange.
It's left to them to find how they might seize bodies for themselves—
his seed body, to theirs—for the bodies to come thronging down
   the bloodline.

If not out of their heads, then into the teeming
midst of them the daughters go, and through to a calm,
the way the roil and clamor of Gomorrah and Sodom

were brought to the silence of empty mountains, desert places,
by those angels that removed them from the common fate.
No need to frame as thought what hums beneath all thinking

its little tunes: why else spared but by deserving?
Not a rescue of the righteous merely but of righteousness itself
and of their sort precisely, the favored blood

in the correct proportion. It's for the best their mother's
removed, who might have meant dilution—pure idea and
idea of purity, all transpiring as intended or

why was it permitted to transpire? That the days shall increase
and have increase. They will breed among themselves.

THE OLD ART

The old art moved from left to right, plotted, knotted up, unknotted,
stopped, turned around, pointed—
well, twirled really,
could just about say anything
but wouldn't just say anything.
Sure that you were listening,
it overheard, speaking prettily, meaning to please whatever else it means,
saying, you have been here, yes? You will come here, no?

It suffered and sinned but only hinted at the tedium.
The old art doubled back, coincided, came around
again,
tethered itself to a history it
would rather have had or would rather not have
had, made up its mind in either case:
it was a good time; it was not so good
a time.

Somewhere quite close or further off
there's revolution, war,
but beyond all that and in the midst, closer yet, deeper in,
there's a person alone,
or two, two together alone,
out of the group of friends, the small circle
made by a series of random encounters of the sort only an evil
genius or a beneficent deity or
an indifferent fate might devise.

For the old art it was origins as much as destinations.
It leapt up when it beheld, and it beheld and leapt
and had the income and the leisure, mostly.
However, the old art raced the body up a hill,
reached the top, heart pounding,
crashed through a shut door, grappled
with the other there—there were others there—and a house.

And the old art rose
to its full height, swelled to the swell of the music
and paid off whomever had it coming, dispensing just
deserts, grand kindnesses—a boon, a boon,
the sudden gravity of our attractions
falling on us,

us, us—
everyone, presumably in Mombasa too,
pretending to be them also, one at a time or more.
The old art never, the old art always,
thrum and hum and tum ta tum,
a great tree branching out from the past.

The old art had wit, biting and bitten,
and wants us better, betterable,
impersonates an officer if necessary,
could and did.
Uncanny, the old art just like—
and like unto, alas, and then adieu the old art.

APOLLO TAKES THE TROPHY OF MARSYAS

after Bartolomeo Manfredi's *Apollo and Marsyas*

> *"Why tear me from myself? Oh, I repent! / A pipe's not worth the price!"*
> *and as he screamed / Apollo stripped his skin; the whole of him / was one*
> *huge wound.*
> —Ovid, *Metamorphoses* 6.382ff
> (trans. A. D. Melville)

The moment's late in the tale and early in
the penalty phase. Paired nooses high on his arms
yoke satyr to straight gibbet of bare tree trunk.
Whoever challenged whom—there's some dispute
among accounts, Ovid's and others'—the mouthy
satyr has a history provoking
deity; arrogance on both sides only
one side's entitled to. But hubris gives
the story form, a body to be driven
to its end, bound for the place of execution
by a route transgression lays out. The instrument
of trespass is the auloi, ur-oboe Athena
invented and flung beside the still waters where
she had confirmed her puff-cheeked image playing
that set the pantheon laughing. So she forbade
the use of what Marsyas found and made
his virtuoso own. The woods resounded
with his piping, and she slapped his face for him.

This first unwisdom, to antagonize
the goddess of that attribute, predictive—
but must endear him to his demimonde
of mestizo brethren. By grief's measure he
is hero to nymphs and dryads—Ovid reports
a river wept, confluent with his blood,
after he loses as is foreordained,
if anything is. It's gods who win the contest
that gods judge. The price extracted for the loss
is something else again. He must have believed
himself the satyr in a satyr play,
a comedy of contest and wager. The stakes
defining genre for him, vague from the start,
though: whatever the winner decides to do to him,
the loser will accept. So, had Marsyas
heard a flirt of levity in Apollo's
tone where there'd been a sneer? And what
a satyr triumphant might do to such a one
could only be imagined in a farce.

As for the music, whatever loveliness
the lesser being might compose, you'd think
the god's would simply be of another order.
Yet Apollo feels the need for getting clever
and adds his singing to the lyre, claiming
the song's equivalence to breath through pipes
when Marsyas protests what refereeing Muses
allow, it seems. Round two, that was, depending
who tells it. Were rules disclosed beforehand, rounds
included? All sources have Marsyas sure
he'd won the first exchange before Apollo's

variations—song or the altogether other
turn when he flips the lyre, plays it inverted:
Try that with pipes, you goaty-stinker, prick-
eared prick-rampant. Screw with me, will you?

Trophy awarded, the trophy taking is
the final round for Marsyas, trussed up
for short cuts and long slicings, the undress
pattern of incision that will get him
out of himself with the least damage done
legs' leggings, arms' sleeves, face's mask,
et cetera. All parts must hang together
in new display, stitching kept minimal,
not to disrupt the aesthetics of the finish,
the illusion of flat entirety, which raw
Marsyas—the remnant bulk of him—almost
certainly should remain aware for long
enough to apprehend himself. And this,
the art and its appreciation, is as
Apollo intends, a realism in full
accordance with the dictates of a god.

Even applied with care, the flensing blade
will likely slip a little deep or shallow—
Apollo's no butcher, an archer rather. The strong
fingers, nimble on the lyre, can hook
and draw flesh back like bowstring. Marsyas helped
off with his coat thus will hang unjacketed:
the reveal, no crisp textbook illumination.
Patches of fatty undersheath might slide
off like the last of snowmelt—wintry vines

of disembedded nerve and vein dangle
over the layered weave of muscle, which must
be deeply breached around the breastplate,
skinning brought to bone, for Ovid to prove
correct about what's visible after: the twin
hives of the lungs aswarm, all the innermost
of flesh shaking as the heart punches
the sides of its small sack, wanting out,
till quickly bloodfall curtains off the sight.

First-blood trickles to the god as pictured
here wearing a laurel crown of outsized leaves.
His left hand grips Marsyas' right forearm,
knife's tip in it, most delicate of right
uppercuts begun. The pale god stoops,
such exact dispassion, intent on bladework
but also on Marsyas, regarding how
he takes this, looking to increase a vengeful
pleasure? But no, Manfredi embodies in
Apollo's face a spirit of pure inquiry.

Whatever he wants to know, the god might have
some answers could he see behind Marsyas'
back, where his left arm curves around the tree trunk,
the flat of his hand bracing him, skin pressed
to bark. He'd see the sole material
resistance now to him is in Marsyas'
integument alone, the natural
reluctance of the skin to be removed.
Nothing is left Marsyas but retractions:
his last outcries of regret, and then what portion

of the self he can withdraw he will, before
it's taken. The back hand like some secret sign
of reservation is instead the clench
of acquiescence, steadying him before
the awful consequences of so little.

The satyr is in the *oscuro* of chiaroscuro.
The shadow on his face the god casts
makes his expression somewhat hard to read.
Manfredi's decorum that would be, this veil.
Despite the wound, it's too early, and too easy,
to feature Marsyas with the gape mouth mask
of extremity, to paint his face the face
of some contorted anyone. No question
shock is discernible in Marsyas' stare,
but he seems thoughtful too. Surely he
could think still, in between surges of dread,
beyond regret, what music was to him.
Before he's changed into an instrument
that ranges castrato shriek to bass moan,
he'll understand at last what he had never
mastered: he will know the way things are.
The contest won, as it must be, by the god
of music, then comes the flayer, administering
agonies, bright Phoebus, god of truth.

L. RECEIVES HONORABLE MENTION
IN LATE MIDDLE AGE

As if he'd always had that hidden aspect
destined to emerge that simply took

a long while coming.
                        L. could recollect
some early signs, childishly close kept,
practically secret, the half-filled sketchbooks
still boxed somewhere.
                        The many later missteps—
the blurred photographs, bizarre collages,
clay effigies that cracked off armature wire
he couldn't have realized then were part of the quest
lately ended,
                    objects rightly discarded
as altogether wrong for what required
after all so little to manifest—

a hundred forty words that tumble down
twelve lines, images
                        launched with the dark-
winged patch that skitters across rough ground,
sweeps up the elm's trunk, rejoining hawk
with shadow, what's alighted
                                with what's risen.

And a life is rescued somehow, his time redeemed
from the waste by what he's suddenly written,
time spent on surfaces
                              when there were depths;
from his inability to make it mean
reprieved, soul-making giving evidence.
Even if he also had to accept
the judges
              missed a lot of what he meant,
he feels at least he has been recognized—
found his one talent that was death to hide.

WHAT MEN WANT

Last plates, small squares, pushed to the center where
the spires of four green bottles tower empty,
the talk between them at the table—three pairs
of men and women, husbands and wives—now turns
to men and women, husbands and wives, and edgy.
So he begins his contribution with
such caution as his current state allows,
an anecdote of several years before . . .
he thinks his wife might possibly recall—
about the way that men will notice women
in the street? She doesn't? Well, it had been

a chance sighting from afar at first,
tracked to the middle distance of a busy
corner crosswalk one blustery afternoon.
He'd sheltered in a storefront from a sun-
shower when he caught a flash of white
legs like . . . like a birch, itself within a fog
of other trees, a blur of limb and trunk. . . .

"Bravo. The masterful observer ever,"
his wife put in, "from your position all
that moved, toward you or not, moved for you."

"I wouldn't yet have had my tendencies
revealed to me. Unreconstructed as

I may have been, still she was someone who
could even draw an eye not on alert
already in that way men have in cities. . . ."

"Just cities?" another of the women said.

"Apparent in the cities where I've lived,
let's say. With your permission. . . . Anyway,
whether seen from far off, mid-distant,
or passing close, it's all sidelong somehow,
at least among those who are civilized
mostly, peripheral carnality
if that, barely sensation, hardly thought.
Looking, we see—"
                              "You see you look, how can
you help it? Nature. Of the visual,
I mean," the longest married husband said.

"—first one and then another, and in them, vaguely,
the shapes of our desire: leg and breast,
a face we'll just have time to judge pretty
or haughty, maybe with the fending off,
before another comes, to unformed thoughts
of touch, the laying on of eye. . . ."
                              "Ach, vaht
do men vant, daht's ze kvestion." This from his wife's
best friend, drawled in her Dietrich imitation.

"What's a man want to see those moments looking
but other lives he might be living—though
he couldn't say, is likely unaware

and has been happy with his own? And when
within the general scan all at once—"
Here he makes a camera of his hands
and shows a pan become a zoom to close-up,
signifying how what's broadcast takes
particular root.
                    "—an instant like one in which
nothing happens resembles one when much can.
Don't we insist romance, lives quicken on
a line of sight, the sudden strike of beginning?
Among a crowd that lovely woman nearing:
the slim ankles, skirt and matching jacket
I hadn't seen before, billowing some,
also her hair, blowing across her face,
freshly cut and styled, its dark cherry
flare the sure giveaway. I had to laugh
to myself at how 'the suit became her,' became
you, my wife of several years by then,
do you remember?"
                    "I remember meeting
by chance downtown a time or two, if not
this story that you made of it, so do
share what you gathered through coincidence."

"I found it funny right off as I say
and maybe something amusing to tell at parties,
but it stuck with me, replaying enough to seem
like more, like evidence—oh, nothing cosmic,
not fate or anything. I dug around
for what, though, starting with I surely must
have known that it was you before I knew

I did—true maybe but beside the point,
the subconscious doing its quick work
underground, but what else was it keeping
to itself, reserved for miners? Up top
I'd almost settled on the irony,
'Beware, the life that you imagine might
well be your own,' a sort of joke on me.
Except it hadn't felt that way at all.
There'd been straight joy (yes, 'straight,' I hear it now)
in surprise, pleasure in seeing you, in seeing
it was you, and in how suddenly this life
of mine—of ours—at any moment might
give itself to be imagined newly."

GRUDGE

The last of a late night's argument,
the dreadful unsnarling of intent—
our *what you said* and *what I meant*
and neither of us penitent,
though nearly ready to relent
in laughter as we get the scent
of our absurdity, each pent
to a bed's edge, when the apartment
takes its turn as the respondent—
the babbling pipes, the sighing vent.
After the hours and anger spent,
what I continue to resent
is how, some sliver of a moment,
sleep comes for you, and for me doesn't.

ATTENTION

Can your performance face the open fields and the seaside?...
Does it see behind the apparent custodians the real custodians standing,
menacing, silent—
—Walt Whitman, "By Blue Ontario's Shore"

Afraid that no one was reading my book,
I went through a period of giving copies away,
often to writers whom I knew and liked,
but I'm not sure they read it either.

Some years before I had a book to give
I heard a famous poet say once that
a friend of his—of equal reputation—
claimed that beneath all our poems lies
a single message—other words pulsing
just below the words,

what all the lines,
the rhythms, the great varieties
of language come down to.
According to the friend, under his
ran the plea: *Like me ... Like me ... Like me....*

This was told to a group
of poets to preface the account
of his own discovery on a government tour

of eastern Europe
in the tones his Bulgarian translator
made of the sounds of his poem.

A dowser's pluck flashed through
him that he was hearing right then what
all the cadences amounted to
or covered for, there in the rhythm
somehow, flowing subterranean

the one phrase, a question, over and over:
Are you listening? Are you
listening? Even this celebrated man, apparently,
even him, worried that no one would,
however lightly the admission

that afternoon, a gathering at another
well-known writer's house someone sublet—
wainscoted and dark,
trade magazine ads posted in the bathroom
from the industry she skewered
in a best-selling exposé.

Routinely, we would extend
"Contemporary Poetic Traditions"
past the morning's formal
study into lunch together
in various assortments,

and reuniting afterwards for more—
impromptu pantheon debate—laureling

and claiming kin with Titans
and Olympians, making our
niche reservations, cleavings to
and cleavings from.

And matinee went to soiree
next—after dinner readings: our own work
delivered to each other among
local friends and guest readers too.

Our seminar director's friend
attended once,
and our director always
as generous with his evening
presence as with his daily brilliance.
Eleven weeks before we ended

with the final class in session around
the massive table, closing minutes,
and he spoke his parting
words for us, not his alone,
a section out of Whitman's "Blue Ontario"

for valediction, the part with
many and stern questions
about what it took to be a poet,
*Who are you indeed who would talk
or sing to America?*—
how the terms were *obdurate*.

What I heard below the lines,
a dark bass hum, say, under his rich baritone
was *not you, few—none*
of you, maybe—not you anyhow.

Not that he looked my way in particular.
He looked around at everyone,
up from the book,
the way a good speaker makes contact,
sweeps eyes over
the faces of the audience

or just above their heads.
He and Whitman, keepers at the gate.
This was what I made of it,
last words minatory,
whatever he meant.